William Cathcart

The Baptists and the American revolution

William Cathcart

The Baptists and the American revolution

ISBN/EAN: 9783337235239

Printed in Europe, USA, Canada, Australia, Japan

Cover: Foto ©Lupo / pixelio.de

More available books at **www.hansebooks.com**

INTERIOR OF INDEPENDENCE HALL.

The Meeting House which John Hart built
for the Baptist Church of Hopewell N.J.

John Hart Speaker

THE BAPTISTS

AND

THE AMERICAN REVOLUTION.

BY

WILLIAM CATHCART, D.D.,

PHILADELPHIA.

PUBLISHED FOR THE AUTHOR.
SECOND EDITION.

PHILADELPHIA:
S. A. GEORGE & CO.
1876.

A portion of the following work was prepared at the request of "The Baptist Ministerial Union" of Pennsylvania, and delivered at their annual meeting in Meadville, October, 1875, when the following resolution was passed:

"*Resolved*, That the thanks of the Union be tendered to Brother Cathcart for his able and instructive essay, and that a committee of three brethren be appointed to confer with the author in regard to the publication and circulation of the essay."

Upon the delivery of the same address before the Philadelphia Association at its annual meeting in October, 1875, the following resolution was unanimously carried:

. "*Resolved*, In view of the part which the Baptists of America took in the formation of our government, and especially in contending for religious liberty, that Brother Cathcart be requested to furnish a copy of his able and eloquent address for publication in the Minutes of the Association."

PREFACE.

BAPTISTS have ever been the ardent friends of civil and religious liberty. Their history in the New World overflows with testimonies of this character.

They have never regarded the military profession with much favor, and, as a rule, have only resorted to arms in great emergencies when the worst evils threatened an entire people. So that we must not look for them among the principal commanders of the Revolution.

The leading men of Massachusetts and Virginia, the two great arms of the Revolution, were hostile to the Baptists, and had lent their aid to laws which grievously persecuted them right down to the commencement of the great

3

struggle, and it is not to be expected that they would place members of the " Sect everywhere spoken against" in prominent military positions.

These oppressive laws kept numbers from uniting with our people, who held their principles; and compelled many British Baptists to stay in the mother country who would otherwise have found a home in America.

Notwithstanding these considerations our brethren acted a glorious part in the conflict, which secured our liberties, and which set the world an example which so many nations have already followed.

This little work is not a history of all the efforts of our Baptist fathers to make the American Revolution triumphant, but a sketch of persons and events precious to our great denomination and dear to patriots of every creed and clime.

CONTENTS.

THE BAPTISTS AND THE AMERICAN REVOLUTION.

It is our profound conviction, and we should, on all occasions, manifest the same, that we should venture our all for the Protestant religion and the liberties of our country.— " Protest of the Messengers of one hundred Baptist churches in London, in 1689."—*Ivimey's History of the English Baptists, III.*, 335.

THE American Revolution secured a fund of glory sufficiently large to give an ample portion to every one who shared in its struggles and sacrifices. Men of nearly every Christian creed, and the author of "The Age of Reason," and "The Rights of Man," aided in obtaining for our country its best temporal blessing, and for the world the richest gift of a beneficent Providence. All Christian communities in the "Thirteen Colonies" labored with quickened zeal to secure our liberties, and they achieved unbounded success.

Denominations, whose principles to-day ac-

7

cord with universal liberty, are not responsible for the persecutions inflicted by their religious ancestors in Colonial times. Nor are modern Baptists entitled to any credit for the glorious doctrines and practices of their fathers in Revolutionary days. But we naturally take a special interest in our sainted and heroic predecessors, whose sacred worth and patriotic deeds have justly earned for them a respectable share of the admiration of mankind. Moved by this consideration, we propose to examine

The Relations of the Baptists to the American Revolution.

When William Pitt stated, in the British House of Commons, May 30th, 1781, that "The American war was conceived in injustice, and nurtured in folly, and that it exhibited the highest moral turpitude and depravity, and that England had nothing but victories over men struggling in the holy cause of liberty, or defeats which filled the land with mourning for the loss of dear and valuable relations slain in a detested and impious quarrel," and when, six months later, in the same assembly, and two days after

Cornwallis' surrender at Yorktown had been published in England, the eloquent Fox adopted the words of Chatham, uttered at the beginning of the Revolution, and said: "Thank God that America has resisted the claims of the mother country!"* and when Burke and others, in the same legislature, spoke words of kindred import, full of peril to themselves, they expressed the sentiments of the Dissenters of England, and especially of the Baptists. When Robert Hall, the future eloquent preacher, was a little boy, he heard the Rev. John Ryland, of Northampton, a man of commanding influence among the Baptists, say to his father: "If I were Washington I would summon all the American officers, they should form a circle around me, and I would address them, and we would offer a libation in our own blood, and I would order one of them to bring a lancet and a punch bowl and we would bare our arms and be bled; and when the bowl was full, when we all had been bled, I would call on every man to consecrate himself to the work by dipping his sword into the bowl

---

* History of England by Hume, Smollett and Farr, III., pp. 155, 162.

and entering into a solemn covenant engagement by oath, one to another, and we would swear by Him that sits upon the throne and liveth for ever and ever, that we would never sheathe our swords while there was an English soldier in arms remaining in America."*

Dr. Rippon, of London, in a letter to President Manning, of Rhode Island College, written in 1784, says: "I believe all our Baptist ministers in town, except two, and most of our brethren in the country were on the side of the Americans in the late dispute. . . . We wept when the thirsty plains drank the blood of your departed heroes, and the shout of a King was amongst us when your well-fought battles were crowned with victory; and to this hour we believe that the independence of America will, for a while, secure the liberty of this country, but if that continent had been reduced, Britain would not have been long free."† This was the spirit of the British Baptists during the Revolution, whose representatives in Parliament, though of another creed, breathed defiance in the ears of the king's ministers.

---

* Robert Hall's Works, Harper, vol. IV., pp. 48-9.

† Backus' History of the Baptists, Newton, II., p. 198. N.

JUST BEFORE THE REVOLUTION THE BAPTISTS GAVE
THE COLONISTS OF AMERICA AN IMPRESSIVE EX-
AMPLE OF DISOBEDIENCE TO WICKED LAWS.

Among the Anglo-Saxon people law has
always had a peculiar sanctity, and precedent
and custom have enjoyed a special reverence.
Other nations in times of excitement have occasionally uprooted their most sacred and ancient
institutions, and swept away every trace of their
existence. But even slight fundamental changes
among populations of Anglo-Saxon origin have
been generally regarded with suspicion, and have
been only adopted after most serious deliberation,
and from a conviction of their pressing necessity.
The Baptists in this country, in 1770, may have
been regarded as fanatics, but they were universally esteemed as men of God who would not
perpetrate what they knew to be a wrong for all
the world. And when they deliberately, everywhere, and very frequently violated the plainest
Colonial laws, and showed a readiness to suffer
anything in their persons and property rather
than submit to enactments in conflict with their
consciences, the attention of the whole people
was aroused, and the wisdom of many of the

2

best men in all the colonies led them to doubt
the patriotism of obeying unjust laws. And
by this painful method the suffering Baptists
trained their countrymen to disregard the tyrannical legislation of the mother country.

In 1770, many of our Colonial law-makers
had a portion of the spirit of Deputy-Governor
Dudley, of Massachusetts, who, when he died,
had these lines, among others, in his pocket:

> " Let men of God, in court and churches, watch,
>   For such as do a *toleration* hatch." *

But our Baptist fathers demanded full liberty
of conscience for themselves, and for all others,
and gloried in disobedience to all persecuting
laws.

In June, 1768, John Waller, Lewis Craig and
James Childs, three Baptist ministers, were arrested in Spottsylvania county, Virginia, on the
charge of "preaching the gospel contrary to
law." "May it please your worship," said the
prosecuting attorney, " they cannot meet a man
on the road without ramming a text of Scripture
down his throat." On refusing to pledge them-

---

* Grimshaw's History of the United States, p. 58, Phila., 1836.

selves to stop preaching in that county for a year and a day, they were forthwith ordered to prison. And as they were led through the streets of Fredericksburg to the county jail, they united in singing the well-known hymn:

> "Broad is the road that leads to death,
> And thousands walk together there;
> But wisdom shows a narrow path,
> With here and there a traveller."*

While in prison for preaching "contrary to law" in obedience to Christ's commands, and in accordance with the promptings of hearts full of love for perishing souls, they proclaimed the glorious gospel to listening throngs through the prison doors and windows. And when they were set at liberty they went forth avowed rebels against these tyrannical enactments on the statute book of Virginia.†

In Middlesex and Caroline counties, Va., many Baptist ministers were imprisoned for preaching; the jails into which they were cast were loathsome with vermin; they were subjected to the treatment of common felons, and

---

* Cramp's History of the Baptists, p. 532.
† Howison's History of Virginia, II., 167-8.

no legal effort was left untried to stifle their earnest efforts to win the lost to the cross.*

William Webber and Joseph Anthony were imprisoned in Chesterfield county for preaching Jesus. And such poor reverence did they cherish for the unjust laws of Virginia that they actually invited the people to come to the walls of the jail that they might proclaim to them the good news of the kingdom.† Colonel Archibald Cary, of Ampthill, according to tradition, was the greatest persecutor in this county; and in it the law outraged the rights of Baptists more frequently and more oppressively than anywhere else in that colony. But so little terror did the Baptists of Chesterfield county feel for the punishments of the law that they cultivated that county more extensively than any other in Virginia and reaped from it an abundant harvest.‡

The Rev. James Ireland was thrust into prison for preaching in Virginia, and while in jail an effort was made to destroy his life by

---

* Howison's History of Virginia, II., 169.
† Ibid.
‡ Campbell's History of Virginia, 555, Phila., 1860.

putting powder under the floor of his cell, but it was unsuccessful; then his enemies tried to suffocate him by filling his little room with the stifling* fumes of burning brimstone and pepper-pods; and finally his physician and jailor conspired to poison him, and though the attempt did not immediately destroy him, yet he never fully recovered from the effects of their atrocious dose.† But neither imprisonment nor threatened or attempted murder could silence this grand old minister or his courageous brethren. To keep the people from hearing the imprisoned preachers a wall was sometimes built around the jails in which they were confined, and half drunken outcasts were hired to beat drums to drown their voices;‡ but they would preach, and the Spirit, as in apostolic times, blessed the testimony of the prison witnesses for Jesus. Baptist ministers were mobbed; sometimes, while they were immersing converts, men on horseback would ride into the water and try to turn bap-

---

* Leland's Works, p. 107.

† Howe's Virginia Historical Collections, p. 239, Charleston, 1846.

‡ Leland's Works, p. 107.

tism into ridicule; they were often interrupted
in their discourses and insulted;* and the law
laid upon them its heavy hand, but they de-
spised the jail, the lash, and the malicious jeer.
And when they were hunted like wild beasts,
and denounced as wolves in sheep's clothing,
they meekly replied, "That if they were wolves
and their persecutors the true sheep, it was un-
accountable that they should treat them with
such cruelty; that wolves would destroy sheep,
but that it was never known till then that
sheep would prey upon wolves."† And they
went forth in violation of law and in contempt
for all illegal opposition to prey upon the un-
converted sheep and to bring all Virginia to
Jesus.

In New England they were frequently arrested
for not paying taxes to support the Congregational clergy, and women‡ were honored with
this privilege as well as men. Their property
was seized, and generally sold for a mere trifle
to pay the church dues of their neighbors of the

---

* Howison's History of Virginia, II., 169, Richmond, 1848.
† Semple's History of Virginia Baptists, p. 21.
‡ Backus' Church History, Newton, II., 97.

" Standing Order." The sacred tax collectors at Sturbridge, Mass., according to an unimpeachable witness, "took pewter from the shelves, skillets, kettles, pots and warming-pans, workmen's tools and spinning-wheels; they drove away geese and swine and cows, and where there was but one it was not spared. A brother, recently ordained, returned to Sturbridge for his family, when he was thrust into prison, and kept during the cold winter till some one paid his fine and released him. Mr. D. Fisk lost five pewter plates and a cow; J. Perry was robbed of the baby's cradle and a steer; J. Blunt's fire-place was rifled of andirons, shovel and tongs, and A. Bloice, H. Fisk, John Streeter, Benjamin Robbins, Phenehas Collier, John Newel, Josiah Perry, Nathaniel Smith and John Cory and I. Barstow were plundered of spinning-wheels, household goods, cows, and their liberty for a season."* Sturbridge is but a specimen of what was occurring all over New England, except in Rhode Island. But our fathers submitted to robbery and loathsome prisons

---

* Backus' Church History, Newton, II., pp. 94–5, note.

with foul associates rather than render willing obedience to iniquitous laws. In the East and in the South Baptist witnesses, from prison windows, and sometimes with scourged shoulders, and in a voice as holy as ever floated on the lips of martyrs, announced to multitudes of men that " Unrighteous laws were conspiracies against God and the best interests of our race, plots of the Evil One, to be met by exposure and stern resistance, disobedience to which was loyalty to Jehovah."

Bordering on Revolutionary days persecutions were more general than ever before, and the testimony of Baptists against the crime of obeying sinful laws was in the very air and floating on the sunbeams of every morning, and when George III. resolved on taxation for the Colonies without representation, the example of the Baptists became contagious, and resistance to this despotical doctrine became the engrossing thought of the Colonists of America.

RHODE ISLAND IS A GOOD EXAMPLE OF THE RELATIONS OF OUR BAPTIST FATHERS TO LIBERTY AND THE REVOLUTION.

Many of the noble sons of Rhode Island, in the "times that tried men's souls," were of other creeds, but a much larger number followed the people, the stream of whose denominational life you can trace through every age till you see it issue forth from the heart of the Great Teacher, stepping up out of the Jordan. Morgan Edwards, a man of great historical learning, who died in 1795, says: "The Baptists have always been more numerous than any other sect of Christians in Rhode Island; two-fifths of the inhabitants, at least, are reputed Baptists. The governors, deputy-governors, judges, assemblymen and officers, civil and military, are chiefly of that persuasion."*

"The first work of the Rhode Islanders," says Edwards, "after their incorporation in 1644, was to make a law that 'Every man who submits peaceably to civil government in this Colony

---

* Collections of the Rhode Island Historical Society, VI., 304.

shall worship God according to the dictates of his own conscience without molestation.'"*

Rhode Island, as early as 1764, foresaw the coming Revolutionary storm, and to secure co-operation among the colonists established a "Committee of Correspondence," whose special duty it was to stir them up to maintain their liberties with spirit and to concert methods for united effort.† On the 4th of May, 1776, just two months before the adoption of the "Declaration of Independence," Rhode Island withdrew from the sceptre of Great Britain, and repudiated every form of allegiance to George III.‡ Scarcely had the retreating troops of General Gage reached Boston from Concord and Lexington when the nearest Rhode Island towns had sent recruits to their Massachusetts brethren in arms; and the Legislature soon after voted fifteen hundred men to be sent to the scene of danger. The people of Newport removed forty

---

* Collections of the Rhode Island Historical Society, VI., p. 304.

† Bancroft's History of the United States, V., 218.

‡ Biography of the Signers of the Declaration of Independence, Philadelphia, 1831, I., 374; Arnold's History of Rhode Island, N. Y., 1860, II., 374.

pieces of artillery from the royal fort to a place of security, where they might be ready for the defence and not the destruction of patriots. When the Declaration of Independence was proclaimed at Newport, East Greenwich and Providence, it called forth the most enthusiastic outbursts of delight, and shouts for " Liberty o'er and o'er the globe."* A British historian says : " The Rhode Islanders were such ardent patriots that after the capture of the island of Rhode Island by Sir Peter Parker, it required a great body of men to be kept there, in perfect idleness, for three years, to retain them in subjection."† Governor Green, in a dispatch to Washington, in 1781, says: "Sometimes every fencible man in the State, sometimes a third, and at other times a fourth part, was called out upon duty."‡ But the little State that had declared its independence while other Colonies were hesitating, and thirty-two days‖ before the brave

---

* Bancroft's History of the United States, IX., 36.

† History of England by Hume, Smollett and Farr, III., 90.

‡ Collections of the Rhode Island Historical Society, VI., 290.

‖ Howison's History of Virginia, II., 133.

and patriotic Virginians had renounced allegiance to the English king, never halted for a moment in her courageous efforts. Her sons, with the blood of Roger Williams and his valiant friends in their veins, showed their American brethren that liberty was the sovereign of their hearts.

Before the Revolution Rhode Island was the freest Colony in North America, or in the history of our race. Her Baptist founders had made their settlement a Republic complete in every development of liberty, even while under the nominal rule of a king; they created a government with which there could be no lawful interference by any power in the Old World or the New. Rhode Island had no viceroy; before the Revolution the king had no veto on her laws. In March, 1663, it was enacted that "no tax should be imposed or required of the Colony but by the act of the General Assembly."* In 1704, Mompesson, the chief-justice of New York, wrote Lord Nottingham that "when he was in Rhode Island the people

---

* Biography of Signers of the Declaration of Independence, Philadelphia, 1831, I., p. 341.

acted in all things as if they were outside the dominion of the crown."* Bancroft speaks of Rhode Island at the Revolution "as enjoying a form of government, under its charter, so thoroughly republican that no change was required beyond a renunciation of the king's name in the style of its public acts."† "Rhode Island," says her historian, Arnold, when the United States Constitution was adopted, "for more than a century and a half has enjoyed a freedom unknown to any of her compeers, and through more than half of that period her people had been involved with rival Colonies in a struggle for political existence and for the maintenance of those principles of civil and religious freedom which are now everywhere received in America."‡ The State of Roger Williams had more at stake in the Revolution than any other Colony; founded by men who loved a wider liberty than their fellow-settlers elsewhere, its people were accustomed to enjoy higher privileges than their neighbors, and the destruction

---

* Sabine's American Loyalists, Boston, 1847, p. 15.
† History of the United States, IX., 261.
‡ Arnold's History of Rhode Island, II., 563.

3

of American liberty by the king threatened
them with heavier calamities than any British
plantation on the Continent. With scarcely
fifty thousand people of all ages and of both
sexes, the Baptist State supported three regi-
ments in the Continental army throughout the
entire war;* an immense number for her, when
it is remembered how many men she had to
employ for local defence. Rhode Island began
the struggle early, and continued inflicting her
heaviest blows till victory rested upon the ban-
ners of the United States all over their wide-
spread territory. And when the Constitution
of the United States was adopted, requiring each
State to sacrifice some of its independence to
form a strong General Government, Rhode
Island hesitated long before she would accept
that grand instrument. The other States,
except North Carolina. before 1789 received the
plan of government devised by the Convention
of 1787. They had, however, never enjoyed full
liberty except during the brief period of the
war, but to Rhode Island full freedom was an

---

* Biography of Signers of the Declaration of Independence,
I., 373.

inheritance possessed for many generations, to sacrifice the smallest part of which inflicted great pain. As Baptists we have reason to thank God for the Revolutionary deeds of our heroic brethren in Rhode Island.

THE BAPTISTS WERE AMONG THE FIRST RELIGIOUS COMMUNITIES TO RECOGNIZE THE CONTINENTAL CONGRESS AS A LEGITIMATE BODY.

On the 5th of September, 1774, in Carpenter's Hall, Philadelphia, the first Continental Con-

CARPENTER'S HALL, PHILADELPHIA.

gress assembled.　The eyes of the whole American people rested upon it, and so did the hearts and hopes of a vast majority of them.　Eight days after Congress first met the Warren Association of Baptist Churches solemnly recognized it as, in a sense, the Supreme Court of the American Colonies, and sent it this appeal:

HONORABLE GENTLEMEN:

As the Baptist Churches in New England are most heartily concerned for the preservation and defence of the rights and privileges of this country, and are deeply affected by the encroachments upon the same which have been lately made by the British Parliament, and are willing to unite with our dear countrymen to pursue every prudent measure for relief, so, we would beg leave to say, that, as a distinct denomination of Protestants, we conceive that we have an equal claim to charter rights with the rest of our fellow-subjects, and yet we have long been denied the free and full enjoyment of those rights, as to the support of religious worship.* . . .

Then follows an appeal for such relief as Congress, by legitimate means, may be able to secure.

The Philadelphia Baptist Association, the oldest body of this character in America, sent a large committee to Congress to aid the appeal of our New England brethren.　Dr. Samuel Jones,

---

* Backus' History of the Baptists, Newton, II., p. 200, note.

in his Centenary Sermon before the Philadelphia Association, at its meeting held in this city in 1807, says: "On the assembling of the first Continental Congress, I was one of the committee, under appointment of your body, that, in company with the late Rev. Isaac Backus, of Massachusetts, met the delegates in Congress from that State in yonder State House, to see if we could not obtain some security for that liberty for which we were then fighting and bleeding at their side. It seemed unreasonable to us that we should be called to stand up with them in defence of liberty if, after all, it was to be liberty for one party to oppress another." * These two Baptist bodies formally recognized the Revolution and the Continental Congress, and they were among the first religious communities in the Colonies to give the sanction of their influence to that great Revolutionary Legislature.

Nor does it detract from their recognition that they wanted Congress to assist them in securing relief from persecution. The conscientious Baptists who would preach, though imprisoned and scourged for it, and who refused to pay taxes to

---

* Minutes of Philadelphia Baptist Association, p. 460.

support the State clergy, though certain to be
thrust into jail for their disobedience, and to
have their property seized and sold for less than
half its worth by the officers of the law, would
have borne the worst penalties ever endured by
saintly sufferers rather than have recognized a
body tainted with usurpation.   The true Baptist
will bear any outrage before he will accept relief
by unholy means.   Never were Baptists more
cruelly used than by James II., King of England.
He was the most defective sovereign in moral
worth that ever polluted a throne.   Becoming
a Romanist, he issued a decree dispensing with
all penal laws against Dissenters and Catholics.*
James had no authority to alter any law of
England.   To secure himself from the vengeance
of the next Parliament he abrogated the charters
of several cities and that of London among the
rest, that he might appoint borough magistrates
who would return pliant members to the House
of Commons.   William Kiffin was the most
influential Baptist minister in England, and he
was a wealthy London merchant.   James sought
to bribe him by making him an alderman of

_____

* Neal's History of the Puritans, Dublin, 1755, IV., 46.

London, an office then held in high esteem and still regarded with great favor; he supposed also that by this act of royal favor the Baptists would be disposed to support his usurpation, even though they well knew that he had only ceased to be persecutor for the special benefit of the Papal Church. Kiffin was brought to the palace, and James made his proposition with as much grace of manner as his natural rudeness permitted, and Kiffin immediately and absolutely rejected it. He knew that James had the might but not the authority to make him an alderman, and he refused an honor that came from usurpation. John Bunyan had spent twelve years of his life in prison for preaching Christ; the laws were still in force that had handed him to the jailer, and James might put them in execution any time, but James needed Bunyan's popularity to aid him in his assault upon the liberties of his people and upon the established Church, and he intimated to him that he had an office for him that would show the world the king's estimate of the illustrious dreamer. But Bunyan turned his back upon the hand that offered him liberty and an office, because it was

the hand of the regal burglar who stole the
gifts which he offered.* The representatives
of one hundred congregations of Baptists met in
London in 1689, and adopted the Confession of
Faith which was subsequently known in this
country as the Philadelphia Confession, and they
issued a protest against a small number of obscure
Baptists who had been persuaded by royal favors
to express approval of the dispensing power
which James had wickedly assumed, and in this
document they declare that: "To the utmost
of their knowledge there was not one congregation that gave consent to anything of that nature,
nor did ever countenance any of their members
to own an absolute power in the late king to dis-
pense with the penal laws and tests, being well
satisfied that the doing thereof. by his sole pre-
rogative, would lay the foundation of the destruction of the Protestant religion and of slavery
to this kingdom."† Kiffin, Bunyan and the
English Baptists of James' day, were worthy predecessors of our American brethren in the Revolution. They would have burned with unuttera-

---

* Macaulay's History of England. Boston, 1852. II.. 177, 178.
† Ivimey's History of the English Baptists, III., 335.

ble indignation and turned away in wrath from any American James II. or from any Congress of Colonial usurpers who would have ventured to offer them deliverance from legal wrongs on a principle that would justify the abrogation of any enactment without the intervention of the lawful representatives of the people. In seeking relief from the Continental Congress, the two most influential Baptist organizations in the land gave that Assembly their formal approval. And there is reason to believe that the sanction of two such respectable bodies, publicly bestowed at a time when doubt and alarm prevailed everywhere, had a powerful influence in confirming the faith of patriots in and out of the first Continental Congress, in the righteous character of its deliberations.

THE BAPTISTS AS A PEOPLE WERE ENTHUSIASTIC ADVOCATES OF THE REVOLUTION.

They had walked through the furnace of persecution frequently, and they received such sustaining grace from the Great Saviour that they were afraid of nothing. The timid and lovers of ease turned from the Baptist fold.

Thousands in it had been recently converted, and they were fired with a first and a glowing love. The whole denomination was overflowing with the same enthusiasm which made the early Christians reckon nothing dear to them but the triumph of truth. Their aid in securing Revolutionary freedom was of the highest importance; difficulties to such men were trifles, opposition only stirred up greater power in them than it controlled. The Baptist, by the inspiration of his renewed nature, and by his heaven-given principles, is a lover of universal liberty. He will not rob a child of its freedom by making it a church member through infant baptism before it has exercised its choice or the Spirit has bestowed his grace; he will not force any man, by law, to give pecuniary or other support to his own religious opinions, nor will he inflict punishment for any supposed heresies. He who holds these doctrines is necessarily in favor of unfurling the flag of freedom over every quarter of the earth, and over every human being who can be safely set at liberty.

The Baptist General Association of Virginia notified the Convention of the people of Virginia that "They had considered what part it would be proper to take in the unhappy contest, and had determined that they ought to make a military resistance to Great Britain in her unjust invasion, tyrannical oppression, and repeated hostilities."* And they proclaimed to the world that " to a man they were in favor of the Revolution."† This action undoubtedly had great weight with the Convention whose delegates voted for the Declaration of Independence the next year in the Continental Congress.

Preachers and people, says Semple, were engrossed with thoughts and schemes for effecting the Revolution. This ardent patriotism led some ministers to become

Chaplains in the Army.

Baptists felt the greatest interest in the soldiers of the Revolution, and having unbounded confidence in the power of prayer they were anxious to have holy men of God with our armed heroes in camps, hospitals, and battle-fields, that

---

* Headley's Chaplains and Clergy of the Revolution, p. 250, N. Y., 1864.

† Semple's History of the Virginia Baptists, p. 62.

they might not only point them to the Divine
Saviour who gives health and healing to the
sick and wounded, and victory in every fierce
struggle, but that they might pray to the Lord
of hosts for success in every deadly conflict.   In
A. D. 603, when Brocmail put his army in order
of battle in front of Chester, in old England, to
defend his people against the heathen king of
Northumbria, Ethelfrid, the ministers in large
numbers stood apart from the army praying for
the success of Brocmail.   When Ethelfrid per-
ceived them he inquired what they were doing,
and on learning their business he ordered them
to be killed first, because they had already commenced the battle by praying to God against
him.*   In this spirit Baptist ministers were
eager to go to the army as chaplains.   Leading
pastors from the East, from the Middle States,
and from the South were with their armed
brethren in all the toils, privations and perils
of the Revolutionary war.

The Baptist General Association of Virginia,
which represented a numerous section of our
denomination, applied, in 1775, to the conven-

---

* Bede's Ecclesiastical History, II., 2.

tion of their State for permission to preach to the army encamped in their bounds. Their request was granted; and they sent the Rev. Jeremiah Walker and the Rev. John Williams to address the soldiers. These were the most popular preachers in the Baptist denomination in the Old Dominion.*

Elder M'Clanahan, a Baptist minister, raised a company of soldiers in Culpeper County for the Continental service, chiefly from his own denomination, to whom he ministered as a chaplain, and whom he commanded as their captain.†

The Rev. Charles Thompson, of Massachusetts, a scholar, an eloquent preacher, and a man of great piety, was during three years a chaplain in the army. Mr. Thompson was deemed such a friend to his country by the enemy that he was arrested and kept a prisoner for a short time on board a guard ship, and then somewhat unexpectedly set at liberty. ‡

---

* Semple's History of Virginia Baptists, p. 62.
† Howe's Virginia Historical Collections, p. 238.
‡ Sprague's Annals of the American Baptist Pulpit, p. 134.
4

The Rev. Dr. Hezekiah Smith, of Haverhill, Mass., at the outbreak of the Revolution, had a church for whose spiritual welfare he was tenderly exercised, and to which he was united by fatherly ties. He was a man of refined and retiring habits, and seemingly the last minister in his State likely to seek a position in the army. But his patriotic ardor was so intense that it tore him from church and family and sent him as a chaplain to the army. In his new position he discharged the duties of his office with marked fidelity; and by his refined manners, wisdom and bravery obtained the confidence of the most distinguished officers in the army. He became the intimate friend of Washington himself, who treated him with unusual courtesy. He served in the army for five years, boldly reproving vice, and encouraging a confident trust in the Great Captain of our salvation. He had a commanding person, and the air of a perfect gentleman. The constable of a neighboring town, to which Dr. Smith had gone to preach, was "a weak and inferior-looking person," but he was full of self-importance; and armed with the authority of the law, he came "to warn the stranger out of the place." But when he saw the imposing appearance of the intruder he was confused and stammered out: "I warn you—off God's earth." "My good sir," said the preacher, "where shall I go to?" "Go anywhere," was the reply; "go to the Isle of Shoals."* But the man of God did not leave God's earth, or visit the Isle of Shoals at that time.

The Rev. Dr. Rogers, of Philadelphia, was the first student of Brown University; and in his day he was a man of celebrity in literary circles and of attractive talents as a preacher. Dr. Benjamin Rush was a member of his congregation, and other persons of culture waited upon his ministry. For some time he was Professor of Oratory and Belles-Lettres in the University of Pennsylvania. An English gentleman speaks of Dr. Rogers, while in Philadelphia, as taking him to the residence of Washington, and says: " When we called the General was not at home, but while we were talking with his private secretary in the hall he came in, and spoke to Dr. Rogers with the greatest ease and familiarity. He immediately asked us

---

* Manning and Brown University, pp. 137-8, Boston.

up to the drawing-room where Lady Washington and his two nieces were."* When Pennsylvania raised three battalions of foot, the Legislature appointed Dr. Rogers their chaplain. He was afterwards a brigade-chaplain in the Continental army. For five years this distinguished man followed the fortunes of the Revolutionary army as an unwearied and beloved chaplain.†

The Rev. David Jones was an original thinker, and he was fearless in expressing his sentiments. He was an educated man ; but he possessed what schools never gave, a powerful intellect. As a preacher he always secured the undivided attention of his hearers, and never failed to instruct and cheer them. When the Revolutionary War began, Mr. Jones lived in a section of New Jersey where Tories made it neither agreeable nor safe for a patriot to reside, especially if, like Mr. Jones, he was an orator capable of moving men by his eloquence, and a brave man to whom fear was an unexplored mystery. So Mr. Jones, believing that he could serve his country better

---

* Manning and Brown University, p. 91.

† Sprague's Annals of the American Baptist Pulpit, p. 145.

than by martyrdom from such hands, removed to Pennsylvania.

In 1775, on a public fast, he preached to the regiment of Col. Dewees a sermon overflowing with patriotism, and with unshaken confidence in God. The discourse was given to the printer and widely circulated over the Colonies; and it exerted an extensive influence in favor of the "good cause."

In 1776, Mr. Jones became chaplain of a Pennsylvania regiment, and entered upon duties for which he was better qualified than almost any other man among the patriotic ministers of America.

He was never away from scenes of danger; nor from the rude couch of the sick or the wounded soldier when words of comfort were needed. He followed Gates through two campaigns, and served as a brigade chaplain under Wayne. He was in the battle of Brandywine, the slaughter of Paoli, where he escaped only by the special care of Providence, and in all the deadly conflicts in which his brigade was engaged, until the surrender of Yorktown. General Howe, learning that he was a pillar to

the Revolution in and out of the army, offered
a reward for his capture, and a plot was unsuc-
cessfully laid to secure his person.   Full of wit,
eloquence, patriotism, and fearless courage, he
was a model chaplain, and a tower of strength
to the cause of freedom.   He was the grandfather of our esteemed brother, the Hon. Horatio
Gates Jones, of Pennsylvania.*

The Rev. John Gano was born in Hopewell,
New Jersey, and possessed in a large degree the
patriotic spirit of the Baptists of that place,
which had so many representatives engaged in
the Revolution; he had great mental powers,
and as a "minister he shone like† a star of the
first magnitude in the American churches."
His power as a minister of eminence was widely
felt, and his labors extensive and successful.
From the pastorship of the First Baptist Church,
of New York, he entered the army as a chaplain,
and performed services which rendered him
invaluable to the officers and men with whom
he was associated.   His love for his country's
cause made the humblest soldier a brother; his

* Sprague's Annals of the American Baptist Pulpit, p. 87.
† Ibid, p. 64.

genial manners and fearless daring made him the special friend of officers of all ranks : while the spirit of the Saviour so completely controlled his entire conduct that his influence over his military charge was unbounded. Headley says : "In the fierce conflict on Chatterton's Hill he was continually under fire, and his cool and quiet courage in thus fearlessly exposing himself was afterwards commented on in the most glowing terms by the officers who stood near him." He himself in speaking of it said : "My station in time of action I knew to be among the surgeons, but in this battle I somehow got in front of the regiment; yet I durst not quit my place for fear of dampening the spirits of the soldiers, or of bringing on myself an imputation of cowardice."* When this courageous man "saw more than half the army flying from the sound of cannon, others abandoning their pieces without firing a shot, and a brave band of only six hundred maintaining a conflict with the whole British army, filled with chivalrous and patriotic sympathy for the valiant men that refused to

---

* Headley's Chaplains and Clergy of the Revolution, pp. 255, 257.

run, he could not resist the strong desire to share their perils, and he eagerly pushed forward *to the front.*"* He preserved his moral dignity as a Christian minister under the most trying circumstances, and by his example, spirit, and instructions, he assisted the brave patriots to endure hardships, to struggle successfully against despair, and to fight with the courage of men who were sure that God was with them, and that ultimate triumph was certain. When we read of the self-sacrifice of men like these we are not surprised that they attracted the attention of Washington, and that he declared that "Baptist chaplains were among the most prominent and useful in the army."† And Howe, in speaking of the preaching and position of captain assumed by Elder M'Clanahan, is constrained to say that "the Baptists were among the most strenuous supporters of liberty."‡ We have reason to bless God for these preaching and praying heroes who followed

---

* Headley's Chaplains and Clergy of the Revolution, pp. 255, 257.

† Manning and Brown University, p. 136, Boston, 1864.

‡ Virginia Historical Collections, p. 208.

the standards of the Revolution through hunger
and cold and nakedness, through retreats,
diseases and wounds, through danger and blood
and victory; men whose faith and prayers
brought success from heaven upon our cause,
notwithstanding discouragements and disasters;
men whose names shall be held in everlasting
honor by their Baptist brethren and by American patriots while human history preserves the
records of generous sacrifices and holy worth.

*Some Ministers served the Revolution in other
Spheres.*

James Manning, D. D., president of the college now known as Brown University, was one
of these. Few men in his day, in his own or
other denominations, wielded a more extensive
influence. His polished manners, his acknowledged learning, his quick perception, his untir-
ing activity, his habit of putting his whole soul
into the toils which occupied his time, and the
modest ease with which he moved in every
society, made him a power wherever he went.
In the Revolution he was the most influential
man in Rhode Island. He states in a letter to

Dr. Rippon, of London, written in 1784: "I think I can say that I never in one instance doubted the justice of our cause."* Filled with this conviction he was ever planning something for the public good, or performing it with unwearied effort and unselfish heroism. His conflicts were not on the field of glory, and yet his services were more substantial than the marches and wounds and victorious efforts of some of his military brethren. And Rhode Islanders regarded him as the sage and patriot of their State in Revolutionary times. When General Sullivan commanded the Continental troops in Rhode Island, three men were condemned to death by a court-martial. Manning had his sympathies enlisted in their behalf, and on making an earnest appeal to the General, he immediately gave the president a reprieve for the unfortunate men, with which he hurried to the place of execution and arrived just in time to save their lives.†

The number of men taken away from cultivating the soil in Rhode Island, and the occu-

* Manning and Brown University, p. 328, Boston, 1864.
† Ibid., pp. 259, 260.

pation of a large section of that State by the enemy, made provisions occasionally scarce. Several of the States had laws forbidding the transportation of food beyond their own limits, so that a supply for the wants of Rhode Island became a serious question. To obtain relief Dr. Manning was commissioned by the governor and council of war of Rhode Island to make an appeal to the government of Connecticut to relax their laws on this point. Dr. Manning attended to the duty imposed upon him and was successful beyond his expectations.*

Once entering the Legislature while it was in session, without any special motive, the members without concert on the motion of Commodore Hopkins elected him to fill a vacant seat in Congress. This graceful tribute to his eminent worth was much enhanced by its unanimity, and by the well-known fact that Dr. Manning aspired to no secular position, however exalted.†

After the establishment of the United States government under the Constitution in 1789, and before Rhode Island ratified that instrument,

---

* Manning and Brown University, pp. 259, 260.

† Sprague's Annals of the American Baptist Pulpit, p. 92.

Dr. Manning and Benjamin Bourn, Esq., were
sent to Congress, then in session in New York,
to present a petition for relief from certain
grievances which affected the ocean commerce
of their State.* By persons in all positions in life
from George Washington down, President Manning was regarded as one of the chief fathers
and founders of the American Revolution.

The Rev. David Barrow, a brother of spotless
character, and of extensive usefulness, held in
universal esteem, not only commended patriotism
to others, but when danger pressed he shoul-
dered his musket and performed good service
against the common foe, and he obtained the
same reputation in the camp and in the field
which he enjoyed in the happy scenes of ministerial toil elsewhere.† The Rev. Daniel Marshall was so strongly identified with the cause
of his struggling countrymen that the British
arrested him, and kept him under guard until
he had an opportunity of exhorting and praying
in the presence of the officers and men, and they
at once set him at liberty.‡

---

* Manning and Brown University, p. 424, Boston, 1864.
† Semple's History of the Virginia Baptists, p. 359.
‡ Ibid.. 372.

The Rev. Oliver Hart was appointed by the Council of Safety, then the executive of South Carolina, with William H. Drayton and the Rev. William Tennent, to travel through the State and expound the principles and claims of patriotism to the people.* The Rev. Dr. Richard Furman was one of the most active and useful patriots in the South, and in recognition of his services he was appointed by the Revolutionary Society of South Carolina and the Society of the Cincinnati to deliver discourses commemorative of Washington and Hamilton, and he was elected a member of the convention that framed the Constitution of South Carolina.†

The Rev. Dr. Stillman, of Boston, was a Christian of great consecration of heart, and lived so much for the better world that few would expect him to take much interest in the temporal affairs of this. But in our Revolution, and in the period when its symptoms foretold its sure approach, such men as Dr. Stillman

---

* Sprague's Annals of the American Baptist Pulpit, pp. 48-9.

† Ibid., p. 162.

5

were everywhere enlisted with their whole hearts in its service. No one in Massachusetts was recognized as a more ardent friend of liberty than the pastor of the First Baptist Church of Boston. In eloquent terms he advocated the doctrines of the Revolution in a sermon preached in 1766 on the repeal of the Stamp Act; and in another in 1770 before the Honorable Artillery Company of Boston.*

As a preacher he had no superior in New England ; among his admirers were John Adams, General Knox, and Governor Hancock, who, for a season, was a member of his congregation. He was one of the twelve delegates from Boston in the convention which ratified the Constitution of the United States, and he rendered efficient help in that almost equally divided assembly in securing a majority of nineteen votes for ratification.†

But our brethren out of the ministry planned and toiled and suffered grandly in the cause of freedom. And conspicuously among this class of Baptists appears the name of

---

* Sprague's Annals of the American Baptist Pulpit, p. 78.
† Manning and Brown University, pp. 136, 404.

John Hart, a Signer of the Declaration of Inde-
pendence.

The father of Mr. Hart was a man of courage and patriotism; he raised a company of
volunteers, which he led to Quebec, and with
them he fought bravely on the Plains of Abraham against the French. The son inherited his
spirit, and was universally regarded as one of
the best men in New Jersey. He was well informed on Colonial and European questions, and
he thoroughly understood the inalienable rights
of mankind. He was held in such high esteem
that he was generally selected to settle the dis-
putes of his neighbors, who spoke of him affec-
tionately as " Honest John Hart." In the social
relations of life he was a man of great modesty
and benevolence, and his highest ambition on
earth was to serve God and promote the best
interests of his countrymen. He had no taste
for political life, and in the conventions of his
fellow-citizens he expressed himself by brave
deeds rather than eloquent speeches. When he
entered the Continental Congress* of 1774 he

* History of Independence Hall, by Belisle, Phila., p. 250.

was about sixty years of age. He resigned from Congress in 1775, and became Vice-President of the Provincial Congress of New Jersey. He was again elected in 1776, and took his place among the patriots and heroes who sent forth the immortal Declaration. It was issued July 4th, 1776. When first published it had only the names of John Hancock as president and Charles Thomson as secretary. Two days before it was given to the world the British landed a powerful army on Staten Island, and to impart greater weight to the Declaration it was signed on the 2d* day of the month after its adoption by all the members and circulated extensively throughout the colonies. Mr. Hart had passed beyond the age of ambition and vigorous activity, and the period of life when men voluntarily make sacrifices or even imperil their property or safety, but he considered nothing but his country's liberty. He owned a valuable farm, grist, saw, and fulling mills; he had a wife and family whose happiness and security were dear to him; his residence was on

---

* Biography of the Signers of the Declaration of Independence, Phila., 1831, III., 256.

INDEPENDENCE HALL IN 1776.

51

the highway of the enemy and his signature
was sure to bring down their vengeance in a
week or two; he knew that everything which
he owned except the soil would be destroyed,
his dear ones scattered, and his life taken if by
the providence of the Evil One he was captured,
and yet he did not hesitate to sign the Declaration of Independence, though it might prove his
own death-warrant, and though it could hardly
fail to inflict the heaviest losses and the most
painful sufferings on him and his. The enemy
speedily found out the patriotism and the happy
home of Mr. Hart. His children fled, his property was wasted, and though an old man
heavily laden with the burden of years he was
compelled to leave his residence and conceal
himself. He was pursued with unusual fury
and malice, and could not with safety sleep twice
in the same place. One night he had the house
of a dog* for his shelter and its owner for his
companion. To add intensity to the bitterness
of his persecutions he was driven from the couch
of his dying wife, whose anguish he was not per-

---

*Historical Collections of New Jersey, p. 262, N. Y., 1847.

mitted to assuage.   But the venerable patriot
never despaired and never repented, though he
saw the darkest days of the Revolution.   His
love of country and sufferings gave him the
warmest place in the hearts of his fellow-citizens.
In 1776 he was elected Speaker of the House
of Assembly; he was re-elected to the same position in 1777, and in 1778 the same honor was
conferred upon him.*   He built the Baptist
Church† of Hopewell and gave it its burying-
ground.   In that edifice he and his family wor-
shipped God till he rested from his earthly
toils and entered upon the joys of the redeemed.
John Hart, the Baptist, in brave deeds and
saintly worth, left a name fit for the illustrious
document that proclaimed to the world our
national birth.   He departed this life in 1780.
A shaft of Quincy granite marks his grave at
Hopewell, on which the following epitaph is cut:

---

* Mulford's History of New Jersey, pp. 430, 444, 456, Camden, 1848.

† The Book of the Signers of the Declaration of Independence, Phila., 1861, pp. 35, 36.

(*Front.*)

JOHN HART,

A Signer of the Declaration of Independence

FROM NEW JERSEY,

July 4th, 1776—died 1780.

———

(*Right Side.*)

ERECTED BY THE STATE OF NEW JERSEY,

By Act approved April 5th, 1865.

JOEL PARKER, *Governor,*

EDWARD W. SCUDDER, *President of the Senate,*

JOSEPH T. CROWELL, *Speaker of the House.*

JACOB WEART,

CHARLES A. SKILLMAN,

ZEPHANIAH STOUT,

Commissioners.

———

(*Left Side.*)

First Speaker of the Assembly,

August 27th, 1776,

MEMBER OF THE COMMITTEE OF SAFETY,

1775–1776.

———

(*Rear.*)

HONOR THE PATRIOT'S GRAVE.

It was dedicated on the 4th of July, 1865, on which occasion Governor Parker delivered an address commemorating his great worth.*

———

* Brotherhead's edition of Sanderson's Signers, etc., p. 331, Phila., 1865.

Colonel Joab Houghton

Had no sympathy with royalty, and no fear
of danger. He had a strong mind, an inflexible
will, and a courageous heart. He saw the
path of duty in a moment, and was unusually
prompt in carrying out his convictions. He
was one of the first* men to advocate the calling
of the Provincial Congress of New Jersey, which
overthrew the Colonial Government, and declared that " William Franklin (the royal governor, a son of Benjamin Franklin) has discovered
himself to be an enemy to the liberties of this
country, and that measures ought to be immediately taken for securing his person, and that
henceforth all payments of money to him on
account of salary or otherwise should cease."†
In pursuance of this resolution, Colonel Heard
arrested Franklin, who was placed at the dis-
posal of the Continental Congress, and by that
body committed to the custody of Governor
Trumbull, of Connecticut, and, in that State,
Franklin remained a prisoner until the war was

---

* Life of Dr. Cone, p. 11, N. Y., 1856.
† Mulford's History of New Jersey, p. 416, Camden, 1848.

ended.* When the State government was set up, Colonel Houghton was among the first members of the Assembly sent from Hunterdon County; and he received one of the earliest appointments as a field-officer in the Jersey troops raised for the defence of the United States. Colonel Houghton was in the Hopewell Baptist Meeting-house, at worship, when he received the first information of Concord and Lexington, and of the retreat of the British to Boston with such heavy loss. His great grandson gives the following eloquent description of the way he treated the tidings: "Stilling the breathless messenger he sat quietly through the services. and when they were ended, he passed out, and mounting the great stone block in front of the meeting-house he beckoned to the people to stop. Men and women paused to hear, curious to know what so unusual a sequel to the service of the day could mean. At the first words a silence. stern as death. fell over all. The Sabbath quiet of the hour and of the place was deepened into a terrible solemnity. He told them all the story of the cowardly murder at Lexing-

---

* Life of Lord Sterling, p. 121.

ton by the royal troops; the heroic vengeance following hard upon it; the retreat of Percy; the gathering of the children of the Pilgrims round the beleaguered hills of Boston: then pausing, and looking over the silent throng, he said slowly: 'Men of New Jersey, the red coats are murdering our brethren of New England! Who follows me to Boston?' and every man of that audience stepped out into line, and answered: 'I!' There was not a coward nor a traitor in old Hopewell Baptist Meeting-house that day."* The annals of the American Revolution cannot furnish in its long list of fearless deeds and glorious sacrifices a grander spectacle than this Sunday scene in front of the Baptist church at Hopewell. Joab Houghton's integrity, honesty of purpose, and military capacity, must have been of an unusual order to have secured for his appeal such a noble response. And the men who gave it must have been nurtured in the lap of liberty in childhood, and taught enthusiastic love for her principles in all subsequent years. But this was the spirit of American Baptists in the Revolution. At home from the army for

* Life of Dr. Cone, pp. 11, 12, N. Y., 1856.

a short time, during the darkest period of the
struggle, he found the whole region around his
dwelling overrun and plundered by the enemy.
The able-bodied men were either away with
Washington or hidden in places of security. No
one ventured to resist the marauding bands of
Hessians who were ready to seize the widow's
mite, or the plate of the wealthy. A large
army was near at hand, making it almost certain
death for those who should offer resistance unless
they were stronger than the powerful foe.
Houghton watched a detachment of these military robbers enter a house, and with a few
neighbors he quietly seized the arms, which
in their contempt for the people of the neigh-
borhood they had stacked outside, and then he
compelled them to deliver themselves up as
prisoners; and this almost in the very presence
of an overwhelming British force, and when the
entire population still living in this region was
sunk in abject terror.*

Colonel Houghton was in the field during the
entire war and rendered courageous help in
many a bloody battle, and secured for himself

* Historical Collections of New Jersey, p. 262, N. Y.

imperishable fame. He was an honored member of the Baptist Church, of Hopewell, and grandfather of the late Spencer Houghton Cone, D. D., of New York.

John Brown,

Of Rhode Island, a brother of the celebrated Nicholas, after whom Brown University was named, was a Baptist, whose record is an honor to the denomination, and an American of whom every friend of liberty might be proud. He owned twenty vessels, every one of which might be seized by the navy of the enemy, and yet, from the very first, he was a frank Revolutionist. When the First Baptist Church, of Providence, wished to erect their present edifice in 1774, John Brown was appointed "a committee of one" to build it. And he reared for them a meeting-house eighty feet square, with a spire 196 feet high, at an expense of $25,000, when materials and labor were unusually cheap. The house is a handsome structure even at the present time; but in that day it had few equals on the continent for size and beauty. Providence then had a population of 4321. Mr.

6

Brown was a man of magnificent plans, and he had the genius to carry them out with success.[*]

John Brown might be said to have begun the Revolution himself. In 1772, a British armed schooner called the "Gaspee" came into Narragansett Bay to carry out orders from the British commissioners of customs, in Boston, with a view to prevent violations of the revenue laws. The "Gaspee" was a continual annoyance to the mariners and ship-owners, with whose business she interfered. On the 9th of June, 1772, she ran aground on Namquit, below Pawtuxet. Mr. Brown heard of it, and he immediately ordered eight large boats to be placed in charge of Captain Abraham Whipple, one of his best ship-masters, and he put sixty-four armed men in them. At about 2 A.M., Mr. Brown and his boats reached the "Gaspee;" two shots were exchanged, one of which wounded Lieutenant Duddingston. "This was the first British blood shed in the war of Independence." The crew and officers left the "Gaspee" very speedily, and Whipple blew her up. Mr. Brown was the last

---

[*] Manning and Brown University, pp. 227–229.

man on board.*   In Bartlett's Colonial Records, during four years, from the beginning of 1776, his name occurs in "important committees, and in connection with various public services twenty-six times; no other name has such frequent mention in Bartlett's volume."†   John Brown was a brave, generous, and large-minded patriot, whose services were invaluable to his country in the hour of her great need.

The Laymen Crowded the Ranks of the Army and Labored for the Triumph of the Revolution with all their might.

And they earned for themselves a reputation for love of country and valor which will never die.   And, in the peaceful scenes of domestic life, the churches labored to provide for the army and to plant the seeds of patriotism in hearts halting between their country and its enemies.   And they cheered the brave men in arms, by sympathy with them in their trials, and rejoicings with them in their victories.

John Adams, of Massachusetts, was, on some

---

* Manning and Brown University, pp. 170, 171.
† Ibid., p. 167.

occasions, the bitterest enemy the Baptists had in Revolutionary days, and yet he gives them considerable credit for bringing Delaware from the gulf of disloyalty. to the brink of which he declares "The missionaries of the London Society for the Propagation of the Faith in Foreign Parts" had brought her to the platform of patriotism.*

On the 19th of October, 1781, the American army entered Yorktown, having received Cornwallis and his troops as prisoners; on the 23d, the Philadelphia Association was in session; that night the tidings of the great triumph came; the next morning at "*sunrise*" the Association met, and overwhelmed with the glorious news, praised God for the victory, and recorded their grateful feelings in appropriate resolutions.† To some Americans in Pennsylvania and New Jersey the capture of Cornwallis was a terrible blow: it meant the loss of everything, including country. But the oldest Baptist association in the land got up by sunrise to celebrate the best

---

* Life and Works of John Adams, by Charles Francis Adams, X., 812.

† Minutes of Philadelphia Association, p. 274.

news that had reached them for six long years
—tidings for which their inmost souls blessed
God. And this was the spirit of the whole
Baptist people all over this broad land.

In the Revolution some thought the Baptists were too Patriotic.

Our brethren in the Revolution were so
devoted to liberty, and as a result of this so
warlike, that a man who believed in non-resist-
ance could not stay among them. Martin Kaufmun, a Baptist minister in Virginia, originally
from the Mennonites, who still believed with
them that all wars were sinful as well as all
appeals to the courts of law, abandoned the
Baptists and formed a little sect of his own,
where only the friends of peace would meet.
There is no evidence that Kaufmun was a Tory.
Some sturdy patriots in the Society of Friends
joined the Revolutionary army, and were
expelled by their respective meetings. After
the war they formed the "Church of the Free
Quakers," whose ancient house of worship is now
"The Apprentices' Library," at Fifth and Arch
streets, in this city. Mr. Kaufmun reversed

their position: he left a militant church to found an abode of peace.* If our fathers erred in the struggles of the Revolution, it was in possessing a superabundance of zeal in their country's cause.

Baptists have Received the highest Commendations for their Patriotism.

Thomas Jefferson was the soundest exponder of true liberty whom God ever made; endowed with rare mental power and full of ardor in the cause of freedom, he had ample ability to enable him to detect the lukewarm and discover the enthusiastic. Writing to the Baptist church, of Buck Mountain, Albemarle County, Virginia, neighbors of his, in reply to a congratulatory address which they had sent him, he says: "I thank you, my friends and neighbors, for your kind congratulations on my return to my native home, and on the opportunities it will give me of enjoying, amidst your affections, the comforts of retirement and rest. Your approbation of my conduct is the more valued as you have best known me, and is an

---

* Semple's History of the Virginia Baptists, p. 188.

ample reward for any services I may have rendered. We have acted together from the origin to the end of a memorable Revolution, and we have contributed, each in a line allotted us, our endeavors to render its issue a permanent blessing to our country. That our social intercourse may, to the evening of our days, be cheered and cemented by witnessing the freedom and happiness for which we have labored, will be my constant prayer. Accept the offering of my affectionate esteem and respect."* This letter was written in 1809. Jefferson's opinion of the Buck Mountain Baptists was exceedingly flattering to their patriotism. He well knew their love for experimental religion, with which he had no sympathy. From his correspondence it is evident that Jefferson was simply an advanced Unitarian, full of sensitiveness to slights on his heretical doctrines, and very earnest in advocating them; and that he should write such an epistle to a Baptist church, only shows that they abounded in their love of liberty. Jefferson had a special regard for

* Jefferson's Complete Works, by Washington, N. Y., VIII., 168.

Baptists. The union between him and them
was peculiar; he speaks in his letters with
scorn sometimes of other denominations, but in
a mass of them, which we have read, there is
not a word unfriendly to Baptists. They loved
liberty intensely, and so did he; and this was
the bond that united the sage of Monticello, and
the followers of Roger Williams. In his complete works there are replies to congratulatory
addresses from the Danbury* Baptist Association, the Baltimore and Ketocton Associations,
and the representatives of six Baptist Associations, met at Chesterfield, Va., Nov. 21st, 1808.
This last body was "The General Meeting" of
the Baptists of Virginia, then representing a
host; to them he says: "In reviewing the history of the times through which we have passed,
no portion of it gives greater satisfaction than
that which presents the efforts of the friends
of religious freedom and the success with which
they were crowned. We have shown, by fair
trial, the great and interesting experiment
whether freedom of religion is compatible with
order in government and obedience to the laws.

* Complete Works, by Washington, N. Y., VIII.

And we have experienced the quiet as well as the comfort which results from leaving one to profess freely and openly those principles of religion which are the inductions of his own reason."* Here the retiring President clearly tells these Baptists that they have been the successful friends of religious freedom, and that he and they together, and their friends and his, had swept away all laws that chained conscience, and put the amendment prohibitory of religious establishments in the Constitution. The Baptists loved Thomas Jefferson. The church at Cheshire, Mass., made a cheese, which weighed fourteen hundred and fifty pounds, and sent it to Washington to President Jefferson, in 1801, by the celebrated John Leland, their pastor, as an expression of the warm regard which they entertained for their great leader in freedom's battles. John Leland was a man of singular ability, independence, frankness, humor and piety. Listening to a sermon, in Virginia, on a very cold day, at the conclusion of which several persons were to be baptized, he com-

* Washington's Complete Works of Jefferson, N. Y., VIII., 139.

posed the well-known hymn, beginning with
the stanza :

> Christians, if your hearts are warm,
> Ice and snow can do no harm;
> If by Jesus you are prized,
> Believe, arise, and be baptized.*

Leland represented the opinions of Baptists
on public questions better than any man living
in his day, and he speaks of Jefferson as having
"justly acquired the title of the Apostle of
Liberty;"† and when he attained the presidency,
he describes him "as the brightest orb in the
greatest orbit in America."‡ No language was
too flattering for Revolutionary Baptists to apply
to Jefferson, and he, with no love for other
denominations except the sect of Dr. Priestly,
cherished a warm regard for our fathers in the
faith. Only two addresses from religious bodies
in addition to those already named, one from
the Methodist church in Pittsburg, and another
from the church of the same denomination, in
New London, Conn., are noticed in his "Complete Works."

Howison, the historian of Virginia, says : "No

---

* Leland's Works, p. 28.   † Ibid., p. 86.   ‡ Ibid., p. 255.

class of the people of America were more devoted advocates of the principles of the Revolution, none were more willing to give their money and goods to their country, none more prompt to march to the field of battle, and none more heroic in actual conflict than the Baptists of Virginia."*

Washington pays a glorious tribute to the Baptists for their Revolutionary sympathies and deeds. In his reply to the "Committee of the Virginia Baptist Churches," which expressed to him grave doubts about the security of religious liberty under the new Constitution, a part of which has been already quoted, he says: "I recollect, with satisfaction, that the religious society, of which you are a member, has been, throughout America, uniformly and almost unanimously the firm friends of civil liberty, and the persevering promoters of our glorious Revolution. I cannot hesitate to believe that they will be the faithful supporters of a free, yet efficient, general government."† With such a

---

* Howison's History of Virginia, II., 170.

† Writings of George Washington, by Sparks, XII., 154-5, Boston.

testimony from the noblest patriot of the human race, we may well bless God for our religious ancestry, and pray to him earnestly for grace, that we may never degenerate in piety or patriotism.

Few Tories can be found among the Baptists of the Revolution.

When the Legislature of Massachusetts, in 1778, forbade the return of 311 public enemies to their government, the historian, Backus, who was acquainted with the facts, declares that not one of them was a Baptist.[*]

The English Government gave twelve million pounds to compensate American Tories,[†] and we doubt if one dollar of this money ever went into the pocket of a true Baptist. In his brief biography of 3,200 Tories, given by Sabine in his "History of American Loyalists," we find forty-six clergymen of one denomination, six of another, three of another, and but one of the Baptist faith. This minister was Morgan Edwards, a man of great ability and general

---

[*] Backus' Church History, Phila., p. 196.

[†] History of England by Hume, Smollett and Farr, III., 174.

worth, but eccentric. He had a son, an officer in the British service, whose position is charged with helping to blind his father's eyes to the glories of patriotism. He gave up the public duties of the ministry while the war lasted, and conducted himself with so much moderation as to save himself from exile during and after the Revolutionary struggle.* Edwards was about to be arrested by Colonel Miles, a member of the First Baptist Church of Philadelphia, but he was notified of his danger and left this city immediately. It is gratifying to know that the most rigid scrutiny cannot discover a second Tory among the Baptist ministers of America. Sabine represents Christopher Sower, of Germantown, in this State, as a German Baptist minister. Sower was a printer and bookseller, and unbound Bibles belonging to him furnished cartridge paper for the patriotic troops at the battle of Germantown. He is said to have lost $30,000 through indignation inspired by his disloyalty in the American army.† He was not a Baptist, but a member of a respectable

---

* The American Loyalists, by Sabine, p. 271, Boston, 1847.
† Ibid., p. 627.

7

German community that has no relations with our denomination. There may be some Baptist laymen hidden in Sabine's long list; it would be remarkable if there were not two or three. But we do not know of a single one. Brethren of other creeds fought bravely for our common freedom, and we shall not object to any amount of glory they may desire to claim, so long as they permit our Baptist fathers to enjoy the position which their unsurpassed fidelity and heroism justly earned.

In the work of the Tory refugee, Judge Curwen, there are the names of 926 persons who fled from Boston, when General Howe evacuated it and sailed for Halifax; there are also the names of many others who were exiled by State laws, Committees of Safety, or their own well-grounded apprehensions; among these persons were governors, judges, subordinate colonial officials, eighteen[*] clergymen, and people of all ranks and occupations. This venerable, gossipping ex-judge of New England, while he lived on British alms, wrote a somewhat copi-

---

[*] The Writings of Washington, by Sparks, vol. III., p. 325, Boston, 1834.

ous account of the persons and objects that claimed his attention. Science, literature, war, politics, theatres, and theology are frequently discussed by the fugitive from Salem. But it is not known that a single Tory Baptist has a place in his numerous pages; nor is there even the hint of a suspicion that one of them belonged to our ancient and honored denomination.*

IT WAS DIFFICULT FOR THE BAPTISTS IN THE REVO-
LUTION TO THROW AWAY THE PROTECTION OF
ENGLAND.

The sovereign was a refuge to the Dissenters in any Colony where church and state were united. Time and again the king, in council, had disannulled persecuting laws and released our fathers from odious oppressions. The first Baptist church in Boston, after assembling for years in private dwellings, erected a meeting-house in 1677, which was closed by order of the General Court of Massachusetts; after some time they ventured to use it again, when the doors were nailed up and a paper posted on them which read: "All persons are to take

---

* Curwen's Journal and Letters, p. 448, Boston, 1864.

notice, that by order of the court the doors of this house are shut up, and that they are prohibited from holding any meeting therein, or to open the doors thereof without license from authority till the general court take further order, as they will answer the contrary at their peril."[*] This was a wicked outrage, and on an appeal being made to the king, in council, he immediately rebuked the authors of this base act, and commanded that liberty of conscience should be given by the Congregationalists to Episcopalians and Dissenters.[†] The town of Ashfield, Mass., was settled by Baptists, and when it had a few Pedobaptist families in it they built a Presbyterian church and settled a minister, and then laid a tax upon the land to meet the expenses of both. The Baptists refused to pay the church bills of their neighbors, to which the constable so unceremoniously invited their attention; immediately the best portion of the cultivated lands in the town were seized and sold for trifling sums to pay their ecclesiastical dues; the house and garden of

---

[*] Hildreth's History of the United States, N. Y., I., 497-9.
[†] Backus' Church History, Philadelphia, p. 121.

one man was taken from him, and the young orchards, the meadows and cornfields of others, and the grave-yard of the Baptists was actually among the lots disposed of. These properties realized only £35.10, and they were worth £363.8. Three hundred and ninety-five acres were unjustly seized at this time from their owners. The orthodox minister was one of the purchasers. This was but the first payment, and a couple of others were coming. This proceeding occurred in 1770, just six years before the Declaration of Independence.* An appeal was made to the king, in council, and the law authorizing this civil proceeding was " disannulled."† In 1691, when that illustrious Hollander, William III., sat on the throne of Britain, he granted a new charter to Massachusetts, in which he increased their privileges, but took away some which they had previously enjoyed. He expressly declared that no law should be made without the consent of the governor, whom the crown appointed, and having received his approbation it could be disannulled

---

* Minutes of the Philadelphia Association, p. 116.
† Benedict's History of the Baptists, p. 420.

at any time within three years after it was
enacted. William, who was a tolerant and en-
lightened king, intended to stop Puritan persecutions in Massachusetts, and he was successful
for full fifty years."* On many occasions the
kings of Britain stopped Colonial persecutions
and sheltered Baptists and Quakers from the
wrath of their American neighbors. It was a
serious thing for our Baptist fathers to throw
away this refuge, this last hope in many a
gloomy day, and trust their religious rights to
men who were executing laws full of tyranny
up to the commencement of the Revolution.
And it was a little difficult to join the same
military company with the tax-gatherer who
had robbed you by due process of law, the constable who had lodged you or your widowed
sister or mother in prison because conscience forbade the payment of a tax to support religion,
or the jailer who had put you in the stocks or
scourged you for preaching Jesus, or with the
justice who had condemned you. But Roger
Williams, a short time after his banishment
among the savages, discovered that the Pequot

---

* Backus' Church History, p. 126.

ROGER WILLIAMS.

Indians were trying to get the Mohegans and Narragansetts to unite with them in exterminating the Massachusetts Colonists, and knowing the immense power of these tribes in that day, he at once notified his former persecutors of their danger, and then having successfully used his efforts to throw the whole burden of fighting the English on the Pequots alone, he saved the men and their wives and their children who had no mercy on him.* And like the great founder of Rhode Island, our Baptist fathers, in Revolutionary days, forgave their persecutors, and in view of great dangers threatening the liberties and lives of their countrymen, stood knee to knee and shoulder to shoulder with patriots of loving and persecuting antecedents, and never gave up the conflict until the flag of freedom floated in undisturbed majesty over the entire territory claimed by the thirteen Colonies.

---

*Collections of the Rhode Island Historical Society, II., 319.

THE BAPTISTS WERE CHIEFLY INSTRUMENTAL IN
RESCUING VIRGINIA FROM THE SCEPTRE OF
BRITAIN.

The leading men of Virginia were the descendants of high-born English families, whose
guiding principle for centuries had been loyalty
to the king. Treason to one of them was the
most infamous crime. They were rigid Episcopalians, and so was the king of England and
most of his influential subjects in the British
islands. The rectors of Virginia were native
Englishmen,* many of whom were specially ac-
ceptable to the gay young Virginians because
they frequented the race course, betted at cards,
and rattled dice like experts. One of them was
president of a jockey club, and another fought a
duel. There could not be a more perfect con-
trast between a large majority of these men and
their successors in the Episcopal Church of
Virginia to-day. But as they naturally con-
formed to the tastes and habits of their people,
and as they were bound to England by birth, edu-

* Howison's History of Virginia, II., 159–60, Richmond,
1848

cation and blood, they were fitted to strengthen the ties uniting the Old Dominion to the mother country.

The planter was by position and hereditary inclination what in Scotland is called a *laird*, a *minor* noble who controlled the dependent portion of the white population by his wealth, and his slaves by force and kindness mixed together; he was born to rule, and he was regarded with feudal reverence from his earliest conscious years. The toiling New England farmer, or the cultivators of the soil in the Middle Colonies, might fight for freedom because they lived among equals, but the great planters of Virginia were the natural friends of the mightier lords of England, and of the British king. They clung to Charles I., who was as unscrupulous a tyrant as ever oppressed any people. He levied taxes without the consent of any representative body of legislators, and in shameless violation of law, and enforced his decrees by that Tudor and Stuart inquisition, the Star Chamber. But Virginia adhered to his cause, and "enacted a declaration that they were born under a monarchy, and would never degenerate from the condition of their birth by being subject to any other government." After the king was executed they acknowledged his son, and retained Governor Berkeley, with a commission from Prince Charles.* And though Maryland recognized the authority of the British Commonwealth, and Massachusetts bowed to its supremacy and prohibited all intercourse with Virginia till† she renounced the Stuarts, it required a portion of a powerful British fleet sent out to subdue the Colonies, under Captain Dennis, to constrain Virginia to acknowledge the British government, and remove Sir William Berkeley.‡ In 1660, Governor Mathews of Virginia died, and the people insisted on Berkeley, who was still in the Old Dominion, resuming the office of governor. But he declined to accept it unless they united with him in recognizing Charles II. "This," says Beverly, "was their dearest wish." Sir William Berkeley, while the king was still in exile,

---

* Howe's Virginia Historical Collections, p. 132, Charleston, 1846.

† Ibid., p. 63.

‡ Howison's History of Virginia, I., 298, Phila., 1843.

united with the Virginians in forthwith proclaiming "Charles II., king of England, Scotland, Ireland, and Virginia, and he caused all processes to be issued in his name. Thus his majesty was actually king in Virginia before he was in England."* The Virginians were surely loyal to royalty in these proceedings, but no one can detect any love for liberty in them. The Stuarts that sat on the throne of England were destitute of all love for freedom, and in no deed showed even the faintest regard for it.

When Patrick Henry introduced his five celebrated Resolutions into the Virginia Assembly in 1765 in connection with the Stamp Act, the men of influence in that body were hostile to any opposition to that tyrannical measure, and were going to let it become a law without resistance of any kind.†

Unaided, Henry made his bold assault on the usurpation of the British Parliament in his twenty-eighth year, and during his first session in the legislature. His fifth resolution was:

---

* Howe's Virginia Historical Collections, p. 133, Charleston, 1846.

† Campbell's History of Virginia, p. 541, Phila., 1860.

" That the General Assembly of this Colony has the sole right and power to lay taxes and impositions upon its inhabitants, and that every attempt to vest such power in any person or persons whatsoever other than the General Assembly aforesaid, has a manifest tendency to destroy British as well as American freedom." After the amendment of the fourth resolution, the first four were passed by small majorities. But the fifth was carried by but a single vote, and yet it was only the doctrine of John Hampden and the Long Parliament and of the American Revolution. "Speaker Robinson," says Campbell, "Peyton Randolph, Richard Bland, Edmund Pendleton, George Wythe, *and all the leaders of the House and proprietors of large estates made a strenuous resistance.* Mr. Jefferson says: The resolutions of Henry were opposed by Robinson and all the cyphers of the aristocracy."*

In a speech of wonderful eloquence and power, Henry advocated these resolutions, in which he used the words : " Tarquin and Cæsar had each his Brutus, Charles I. his Cromwell, and George III."—"Treason !" shouted the speaker; " trea-

* Campbell's History of Virginia, pp. 541-2.

8

son, treason," was echoed round the house, while Henry, fixing his eyes on the speaker, continued without faltering,—"may profit by their example."* The next day the men who voted for the fifth resolution, alarmed for their presumptuous deed, actually had it expunged from the journals of the House.†

In Connecticut, the stamp-officer, Ingersoll, was taken in charge by five hundred men on horseback, each bearing a long white pole, from which the bark had just been stripped, and by these five hundred arguments they persuaded him to resign, and to throw his hat into the air and shout three times, "Liberty and property."‡ Elsewhere vigorous opposition was shown to the execution of the despotical Stamp Act. But the leaders of the powerful families of Virginia denounced Henry's fifth resolution, containing the doctrine of the American Revolution: No taxation without representation; which was intended to rebuke the authors of the Stamp Act; with boisterous indignation they made their

---

* Bancroft's History of the United States, V., 277.

† Howison's History of Virginia, II., 52, Richmond, 1848.

‡ Bancroft's History of the United States, V., 318-320.

house ring with cries of "Treason," when he nobly advocated his glorious resolution, and they succeeded, the very next day, in alarming those who voted for it, and in securing its erasure from the records of the House.

How, then, did Virginia take her place in the list of States that fought so bravely for freedom? If, just ten years before the Revolution, her foremost citizens were "strenuously" opposed to the doctrine that there should be no taxes, without the consent of those who were to pay them, it is a matter of great interest to know how they changed their minds.

In Great Britain, perhaps forty years ago, both houses of the British Praliament were filled with land-owners who had legal possession of, probably, four-fifths of the soil in England, Ireland, and Scotland. They had made laws to keep out foreign grain, until wheat reached a certain price in their own markets; and this price would enable them to secure a high rent for their lands. Corn laws were the most important articles in the political creed of a majority of the aristocracy of Great Britain, and they were determined not to repeal them. The

people of England took a different view of the
matter, and felt that they had to pay an extra
price for every loaf to secure for the landlord an
extravagant rent; and they commenced to
agitate against the corn laws; they held meetings in every direction, attended by 50,000,
70,000 and 100,000 men, many of whom were
often hungry; and Sir Robert Peel, a warm
advocate of the corn laws, at last, was persuaded
that he and his Tory friends must repeal those
laws, lest the British constitution should be
annulled, and the throne overturned; and it is
more than probable that loyalty to Britain, in
Virginia, was chiefly destroyed in the same way.

In 1774, according to Howison, "The Baptists increased on every side; if one preacher
was imprisoned, ten arose to take his place; if
one congregation was dispersed, a larger assembled on the next opportunity. The influence
of the denomination was strong among the common people, and was beginning to be felt in
high places. In two points they were distinguished: first, in their love of freedom; and,
secondly, in their hatred of the church establishment. They hated, not its ministers, but its

principles. To a man they were united in the resolve never to relax their efforts until it was utterly destroyed."* These religious descendants of men who had suffered for truth in every country of Europe, and in every age of persecution, since Stephen's blood was shed, were among the most fearless heroes and earnest men the world ever saw. They would journey any distance, and make any sacrifice of time, property, or liberty, to spread their principles; and, though at first treated with insults by the masses, they had now secured so many of the common people in their ranks, and the remainder had become so convinced of the justice of their views about a free state and a free church, that, practically, the Baptists controlled the larger number of white Virginians, whom they led directly into the Revolution; for, to a man, they were in favor of it. At the Revolution, according to Jefferson, two-thirds of the people were Dissenters;† these were composed chiefly of Baptists and Presbyterians; but while the Presbyterians had men of eminent worth,

---

* Howison's History of Virginia, II., 170, Richmond, 1848.
† Jefferson On the State of Virginia, p. 169, Richmond.

they were few in comparison with the Baptists. Patrick Henry found them his lifelong friends, and he would journey any distance to serve them. He rode fifty miles, to Fredericksburg, to be present at the trial of John Waller, Lewis Craig, and James Childs, who were indicted for the crime of " preaching the gospel contrary to law," whose acquittal he speedily secured.* " In their efforts to avail themselves of the Toleration Act," says Campbell, " they found Patrick Henry ever ready to step forward in their behalf: and he remained through life their unwavering friend."† And they applauded all his eloquence for patriotism, and spread over the whole Colony until their country became uncomfortable to Tory Virginians, and the repeated aggressions of the British made it needful to give up Virginia or their political opinions; and the majority of the planters became the friends of a free country.

Had not the Baptists planted their love of liberty in the hearts of the common people of Virginia, had they left them to the teachings of

---

* Howison's History of Virginia, p. 168, Richmond, 1848.
† History of Virginia, Phila., 1860, p. 555.

Tory rectors from British universities, and *lairds* educated in English schools, the descendants of the men who lamented the death of Charles I., and resisted the authority of the Parliament till its fleet compelled their obedience, some of whom were the very men who expunged Patrick Henry's fifth resolution from the journals of the House of Assembly, it is more than probable would have kept Virginia loyal to England in the Revolutionary struggle, and if she had been, every Southern Colony would have stood by her side. And, if the struggle had been confined to New England, without Washington on Dorchester Heights, or warm wishes and material encouragements from southern communities, however bravely our eastern friends might have fought, and they showed themselves men of valor in the field, it would have ended speedily, and most probably in a torrent of Massachusetts blood vainly shed.

Without the Baptists of Virginia, the genius and glory of Washington might have been buried in the quiet home of an almost unknown Virginian planter. The English might not have had to evacuate Boston; our country

MEMORIAL HALL.

90

might have been still in Colonial bondage with ten millions of people, and no great cities; and instead of being the refuge and admiration of all nations, we might have been an obscure and feeble section of a great transatlantic empire. And we should not then have had a glorious Centennial.

BAPTISTS WERE INFLUENTIAL IN SECURING THE ADOPTION OF THE CONSTITUTION OF THE UNITED STATES.

It is a matter of surprise to-day that the wisdom of this instrument was ever doubted, or that it should ever have been opposed by any number of intelligent and patriotic men. The two great States that supported the Revolution were nearly equally divided about the Constitution; and some of the best men in these powerful centres of political life regarded it with unmixed alarm, and resisted it with all their influence and eloquence.

In Massachusetts, the Convention called to ratify the Constitution assembled on the 9th of January, 1788. It was composed of nearly four hundred members. It possessed much of the

intellect and the patriotism of the State. The
parties for and against the Constitution were
about equal. The debates lasted for a month,
and the contest was carried on with great
earnestness.* The entire United States took the
deepest interest in the deliberations. It was
universally felt, as Dr. Manning expressed it,
that "Massachusetts was the hinge on which
the whole must turn," and that if she rejected
the Constitution it would be discarded in the
other States. The Baptists held the balance of
power in the Convention, and they were generally opposed to the Constitution in Massachusetts. The Baptist delegates were chiefly
ministers who had the highest regard for Dr.
Manning. And he, fully convinced that nothing but the new Constitution could save the
country from anarchy, spent two weeks in
attendance upon the Convention, and he and
Dr. Stillman exerted themselves to the utmost
to persuade their brethren to support the Constitution. With the Rev. Isaac Backus, the fearless friend of the Baptist cause, and of liberty
of conscience, they set out, and they met with
success in several cases. And the Constitution

* The prohibition of religious tests in the Constitution
made it many enemies in Massachusetts, Backus II., 335.

was adopted by a majority of nineteen votes. There were 187 yeas and 168 nays on the last day of the session, and before " the final question was taken, Governor Hancock, the president, invited Dr. Manning to close the solemn convocation with thanksgiving and prayer." Dr. Manning addressed the Deity in a spirit glowing with devotion, and with such lofty patriotism that every heart was filled with reverence for God and admiration for his servant. And such an effect was produced by this prayer that, had it not been for the " popularity of Dr. Stillman, the rich men of Boston would have built a church for Dr. Manning."* There is a strong probability that the Baptists of the Convention would have followed Isaac Backus, and changed the insignificant majority into a small minority, if it had not been for Manning and Stillman.

In Virginia, the opposition to the Constitution was led by more popular men; but the parties, otherwise, were about equal in strength. The Convention met in Richmond, in June, 1788. The most illustrious men in the State were in

---

* Manning and Brown University, pp. 103-4, Boston, 1864.

it.   Patrick Henry spoke against the Constitution with a vehemence never surpassed by himself on any occasion in his whole life, and with
a power that was sometimes overwhelming.
Once, while this matchless orator was address-
ing the Convention, a wild storm broke over
Richmond; the heavens were ablaze with light-
ning, the thunder roared, and the rain came
down in torrents; at this moment Henry seemed
to see the anger of heaven threatening the State,
if it should consummate the guilty act of adopting the Constitution, and he invoked celestial
witnesses to view and compassionate his dis-
tracted country in this grand crisis of her history.   And such was the effect of his speech on
this occasion, that the Convention immediately
dispersed.*   The Convention, when the final
vote on ratification was taken, only gave a majority of ten in favor of the Constitution.
Eighty-nine cast their votes for it, and seventy-
nine against† it.   James Madison possessed the
greatest influence of any man in the Conven-

* Howison's History of Virginia, II., 326, 327, 332.
† Howe's Virginia Historical Collections, p. 124, Charleston, 1846.

tion; ·had he not been there, Patrick Henry
would have carried his opposition triumphantly.
And Madison was there by the generosity of
John Leland, the well-known and eccentric
Baptist minister. Madison remained in Philadelphia three months, with John Jay and Alex-
ander Hamilton, preparing the articles which
now make up "the Federalist;" this permitted
Henry and others to secure the public attention
in Virginia, and, in a large measure, the public
heart. Henry's assertion, that the new Constitution "squinted towards monarchy," was
eagerly heard and credited by many of the best
friends of freedom; and when Madison came
home he found Leland a candidate for the
county of Orange, the constituency which he
wished to represent, with every prospect of
success, for Orange was chiefly a Baptist county.
Mr. Madison spent half a day with John Leland,
and the result of this interview was that Leland
withdrew and exerted his whole influence in
favor of Madison, who was elected to the Convention, and, after sharing in its fierce debates,
he was just able to save the Constitution of the
United States. In a eulogy pronounced on

9

James Madison, by J. S. Barbour, of Virginia, in 1857, he said "That the credit of adopting the Constitution of the United States properly belonged to a Baptist clergyman, formerly of Virginia, named Leland: 'If,' said he, 'Madison had not been in the Virginia Convention, the Constitution would not have been ratified, and, as the approval of nine States was necessary to give effect to this instrument, and as Virginia was the ninth State, if it had been rejected by her the Constitution would have failed (the remaining States following her example), and it was through Elder Leland's influence that Madison was elected to that convention."* It is unquestionable that Mr. Madison was elected through the efforts and resignation of John Leland, and it is all but certain that that act gave our country its famous Constitution.

---

* Sprague's Annals of the American Baptist Pulpit, p. 179.

BAPTISTS WERE THE CHIEF INSTRUMENTS IN COMPLETING THE CONSTITUTION OF THE UNITED STATES, THE CHARTER OF REVOLUTIONARY LIBERTY, BY ADDING THE AMENDMENT SECURING FULL RELIGIOUS FREEDOM.

The first amendment to the United States Constitution was adopted in 1789, the year it went into operation. It reads: " Congress shall make no law respecting an establishment of religion, or prohibiting the free exercise thereof, or abridging the freedom of speech or of the press, or the rights of the people peaceably to assemble and to petition the Government for a redress of grievances." The first clause of this amendment occupies properly its prominent place in that addition to the Constitution. Without it the remaining parts would have appeared as lacking in seriousness. The idea that free speech, a free press, a free discussion of grievances and the right of petition were in danger in a country just victoriously emerging from a protracted war in defence of Liberty, could not be deliberately entertained by reflecting persons; and yet, when religious freedom is to receive Constitutional protection, these other

links in the chain of liberty are appropriately
joined to it. But freedom of conscience was
in legal bondage, in 1789, and its friends had
too much cause to be alarmed for its safety.
An absolute necessity rested upon them to
deliver religion from the tyrannical enactments
which then fettered her, and by Constitutional
prohibition guard her from slavery in the future.
The passage of this amendment by Congress
and the Legislatures ultimately but indirectly
destroyed the union between Church and State
in the United States.

But suppose it had not been adopted; Massachusetts might have had her State Church to-
day, and her citizens rotting in prison because
they could not conscientiously pay a church
tax; and any State might have established the
Episcopal Church and then committed Baptists
or other ministers to prison, as they did in
Virginia down to the Revolution. And Congress
might have decreed that the Catholic Church
was the religious fold of the nation, and might
have levied taxes to support her clergy, and
made laws to give secular power to her cardinals,
archbishops, bishops and priests over our schools,

religious opinions and personal freedom. With the amendment we have been educated to practise universal religious freedom; without it sacerdotal tyranny might have destroyed all our liberty. The grandest feature of our Constitution is the first clause of the first amendment. The Baptists have always claimed that the credit for this amendment belongs chiefly to them. It is in strict accordance with their time-honored maxim: The major part shall rule in civil things only.

Where could it have come from? In the Revolution and for a few years after there were two great centres of political influence in our country, around which the other States moved with more or less interest—Massachusetts and Virginia. Freedom of conscience could not come from Massachusetts; she was wedded to a State religion in 1789, which defied any divorcing agency to create a separation. Just ten years before, she adopted her new Constitution, and to secure an article in it giving legal support to Congregational ministers, John Adams, her favorite son, and the future President of the United States, accused the Baptists of sending a delegate to Philadelphia to break up the Continental Congress by creating dissensions about State taxes for ministers. And, after exciting the indignation of the Convention against the Baptists for plotting such a calamity, he represented them as the great advocates of the heresy of separating Church and State, and as the parties to be benefited by this departure from the ways of their fathers; and through this odious misrepresentation Adams had no trouble in fastening the Church to the State, as in the good old Puritan times. And this tie only perished in 1834.* Writing to Benjamin Kent, he says: "I am for the most liberal toleration of all denominations, but I hope Congress will never meddle with religion further than to say their own prayers. . . . *Let every Colony have its own religion without molestation.*"† That is, from Congress; he wished every Colony to have its own *established* church without molestation, if it desired such an institution. He unjustly charged Israel Pemberton, a Quaker, whom, with the Baptists and other Friends, the

---

* Backus' Church History, Philadelphia, p. 197.

† Life and Works of John Adams, by Charles Francis Adams, IX., 402.

Massachusetts delegates met, during the sessions of the first Continental Congress, with an effort to destroy the union and labors of Congress, because he plead for the release of Baptists and Quakers imprisoned in Massachusetts for not paying the ministers' tax, and for the repeal of their oppressive laws. And John Adams actually argued that it was against the con- sciences of the people of his State to make any change in their laws about religion, even though others might have to suffer in their estates or by imprisonment to satisfy Mr. Adams and his *conscientious* friends. And he declared that they might as well think they could change the movements of the heavenly bodies as alter the religious laws of Massachusetts.* This was the spirit of New England when the first amend- ment was proposed, except among the Baptists and the little community of Quakers. Thomas Jefferson, writing to Dr. Rush, says: "There was a hope confidently cherished, about A. D. 1800, that there might be a State Church throughout the United States, and this expecta-

---

* Life and Works of John Adams, by Charles Francis Adams, vol. II., 399.

tion was specially cherished by Episcopalians and Congregationalists."* This was the sentiment of not a few New England Pedobaptists, and the hope of the remains of the Episcopal Church in the South. Massachusetts and her allies had no love for the first amendment.†

It came from Virginia, and chiefly from Baptists of the Old Dominion. The "Mother of Presidents" was the mother of the glorious amendment. In 1776 the first Republican Legislature of Virginia convened, and after a violent contest, daily renewed, from the 11th of October to the 5th of December, the *Acts of Parliament* were repealed which rendered any form of worship criminal. Dissenters were exempted from all taxes to support the clergy, and the laws were *suspended* which compelled Episcopalians to support their own church. But it was the pressure of Dissenters without that forced this legislation on the Assembly, for a majority of the members were Episcopalians.‡ While this act relieved Baptists, the unrepealed com-

---

* Memoirs, Correspondence, etc., Charlottesville, 1829, III., 341.

† According to Backus, Massachusetts *did not* adopt the religious amendment. II., 341.

‡ Ibid., I., 32.

mon law still punished with dismissal from all offices for the first offence, those who denied the Divine existence, or the Trinity, or the truth of Christianity; and for the second, the transgressor should be rendered incapable of suing or of acting as guardian, administrator, or executor, or of receiving a legacy, and, in addition, should be imprisoned for three years.[*] These persecuting laws were not repealed till 1785. The tithe law, after being agitated frequently in every session and annually suspended, was repealed in 1779. The Presbyterians and Baptists were the outside powers that swept away the State Church of Virginia.

After tithes ceased to be collected, a scheme known as the "Assessment" was extensively discussed in Virginia by Episcopalians and others. The assessment required every citizen to pay tithes to support his minister, no matter what his creed. The Episcopalians warmly advocated the assessment. The united clergy of the Presbyterian church petitioned for it,[†] though

---

[*] Jefferson's Notes on the State of Virginia, Richmond, 1853, p. 169.

[†] Rives' Life and Times of James Madison, I., 601-2.

many of their people disliked and denounced it.
Patrick Henry aided it with all the power of
his eloquence;* Richard Henry Lee, the most
polished orator in the country, John Marshall,
the future Chief-Justice of the United States,
and George Washington himself advocated it.†
The Baptists directed their whole forces against
it, and poured petitions into the legislature for its
rejection. The following lines accompanied one
of the Baptist petitions; they were addressed:
"To the Honorable General Assembly," as

THE HUMBLE PETITION OF A COUNTRY POET.

> Now liberty is all the plan,
> The chief pursuit of every man,
> Whose heart is right, and fills the mouth
> Of patriots all, from north to south;
> May a poor bard, from bushes sprung,
> Address your honorable House
> And not your angry passions rouse.
>
> Hark! for a while your business stop;
> One word into your ears I'll drop:
> No longer spend your needless pains,
> To mend and polish o'er our chains,
> But break them off before you rise,
> Nor disappoint our watchful eyes.

* Wirt's Life of Patrick Henry, Hartford, p. 263.
† Rives' Life and Times of James Madison, I., 601-2.

What say great Washington and Lee?
"Our country is and must be free!"
What say great Henry, Pendleton,
And liberty's minutest son?
'Tis all one voice—they all agree,
"God made us and we must be free!"
Freedom we crave with every breath,
An equal freedom or a death.

The heavenly blessing freely give,
Or make an act we shall not live.
Tax all things; water, air and light,
If need there be; yea, tax the *night*,
But let our brave heroic minds
Move freely as celestial winds.

Make vice and folly feel your rod,
But leave our consciences to God:
Leave each man free to choose his form
Of piety, nor at him storm.

And he who minds the civil law,
And keeps it whole without a flaw,
Let him just as he pleases, pray,
And seek for heaven in his own way;
And if he miss, we all must own,
No man is wronged but he alone.*

After expending every effort the friends of
the assessment were defeated, and it was finally
rejected in 1785, and all the laws punishing

---

* Howe's Virginia Historical Collections, p. 381, Charleston, 1846.

opinions repealed. This was a work of great magnitude. The Episcopalians, the Methodists, the Presbyterian clergy and the eloquence and influence of some of the greatest men the United States ever had or will have, were overcome by the Baptists, and Jefferson and Madison, their two noble allies, and some Presbyterian and other laymen. Semple truly says: "The inhibition of the general assessment may, in a considerable degree, be ascribed to the opposition made to it by the Baptists. They were the only sect which plainly remonstrated against it. Of some others it is said that the laity and ministry were at variance upon the subject so as to paralyze their exertions for or against the bill."*

Nor need any one dream that Jefferson and Madison could have carried this measure by their genius and influence. They were opposed by many men whose transcendent services, or unequalled oratory, or wealth, position, financial interests, or intense prejudices would have enabled them easily to resist their unsupported assaults. Like a couple of first-class engineers

---

* Semple's History of the Virginia Baptists, p. 72-3.

on a "tender," with a train attached but no locomotive, would Jefferson and Madison have appeared without the Baptists. They furnished the locomotive for these skilful engineers which drew the train of religious liberty through every persecuting enactment in the penal code of Virginia.

In 1790, just one year after the adoption of the amendment, Dr. Samuel Jones, of Pennsylvania, states that there were 202 Baptist churches in that State.* Semple, the historian of the Virginia Baptists, says, that, in 1792, "The Baptists had members of great weight in civil society; their congregations became more numerous than those of any other Christian sect."† The Baptists outnumbered all the denominations in Virginia, in all probability, in 1789, and they far surpassed them in the burning enthusiasm which persecution engenders; and to them chiefly was Virginia indebted for her complete deliverance from persecuting enactments.

In 1789, a few months after Washington be-

---

* Minutes of Philadelphia Baptist Association, p. 459.
† History of the Virginia Baptists, p. 39.

10

came President, " The Committee of the United Baptist Churches of Virginia" presented him an address written by John Leland, marked by felicity of expression and great admiration for Washington, in which they informed him that their religious rights were not protected by the new Constitution. The President replied that he would never have signed that instrument had he supposed that it endangered the religious liberty of any denomination, and if he could imagine even now that the government could be so administered as to render freedom of worship insecure for any religious society, he would immediately take steps to erect barriers against the horrors of spiritual tyranny.* Large numbers were anxious about the new Constitution, and it had many open enemies. The Baptists who presented this address controlled the government of Virginia, and they were the warmest friends of liberty in America. They will suffer anything for their principles, and as they suspect the new Constitution, it must be amended to embrace their soul liberty, and

---

* Writings of George Washington, by Sparks, XII., 154–5, Boston.

secure their hearty support. A few weeks later James Madison, the special friend of Washington, who aided him five months before in composing his first inaugural address to Congress,* rises in the House of Representatives and proposes the religious amendment demanded by the Baptists, with other emendations, and declares that "a great number of their constituents were dissatisfied with the Constitution, among whom were many respectable for their talents and their patriotism, and respectable for the jealousy which they feel for their liberties." This language applies to his Baptist constituents and their co-religionists over the land. He presses his scheme amidst violent opposition, and Congress passes it. Two-thirds of the State Legislatures approve of it, and it is a part of the Constitution.†

Denominationally, no community asked for this change in the Constitution but the Baptists. The Quakers would probably have petitioned for it if they had thought of it, but they did not. John Adams and the Congregational-

---

* Rives' Life and Times of James Madison, III., 64.
† Ibid., III., 39.

INDEPENDENCE HALL IN 1876.

110

ists did not desire it, the Episcopalians did not wish for it, it went too far for most Presbyterians in Revolutionary times, or in our own days when we hear so much about putting the Divine name in the Constitution. The Baptists asked it through Washington; the request commended itself to his judgment and to the generous soul of Madison, and to the Baptists, beyond a doubt, belongs the glory of engrafting its best article on the noblest Constitution ever framed for the government of mankind.

CONCLUSION.

The Baptists, through William Carey, have given modern missions to the Christian nations. Through Roger Williams the Baptists founded the first State on earth where absolute liberty of conscience was established. Through a letter issued by the Rev. Joseph Hughes, a Baptist minister, advocating the establishment of a society to circulate Bibles, a meeting was held in London, May 4th, 1804, at which the British and Foreign Bible Society was founded, and through it, indirectly, every Bible society on earth.* Through the Rev. John Canne's

---

* Ivimey's History of the English Baptists, II., 93.

HORTICULTURAL HALL.

112

twenty-one years of toil, marginal references were first placed in the English Bible,* and Canne was a Baptist minister. And, as a people, we took a leading part in securing and perfecting American freedom. Our liberty is now shaking all the nations of the earth. It has blessed every section of the mother country, rapidly falling into despotism one hundred years ago. It has torn down the old throne of the Bourbons in France and all the tyrannies that succeeded it. It has banished the petty oppressors that cursed Italy for centuries, and restored some measure of her ancient liberty to the former mistress of the nations. It has bestowed some gifts upon Austria and Germany. It has tried many times to bless the land that gave birth to St. Dominic, Torquemada and Ignatius Loyola. It has reached far distant Japan, and already it is breathing freedom upon its ingenious people. And it will march onward in its career of victory until it breaks the sceptre of the last despot, and the chains of the last victim of royal caprice on the face of the earth.

In unbinding the chains of American liberty,

* Neal's History of the Puritans, Dublin, 1755, II., 50.

and in sending her forth to bless our country and exalt all nations, the Baptists occupied a place conspicuous for its toils and its triumphs. Long before 1776 they had all the seeds of American Independence. They were the seed-bearers of the Revolution, who scattered the seed in every direction and cultivated it under a burning sun. Jefferson was the statesman of the Revolution, Franklin was its sage, Patrick Henry was its tongue of fire, Washington was its sword, Hancock, Hamilton, Adams, Madison, Richard Henry Lee and Jonathan Trumbull were its apostles, and the American people of all creeds and classes were its warriors. May the temple of our country's liberties, reared by the hands of heroes, cemented by the blood of the nation's noblest sons, survive the decay of ages, hurl back the assailing forces of corruption, and continue the admiration of the nations until the recording angel ceases to watch the events of time.

Our country is a miracle of progress unmatched in the annals of mankind, and its greatness is the fruit of Independence. And as every grace in man comes from God, and all his temporal

MAIN BUILDING.

blessings, we will unite with holy John, and say : "Unto Him that loved us and washed us from our sins in his own blood, and hath made us kings and priests unto God and his Father, unto him be glory and dominion for ever and ever.   Amen."

THE END.